A Glimpse

A GLIMPSE

J BRIAN ANDERSEN

ISBN 979-8-9872506-1-7

Cover art: *Prehistoric Blood* by Abel Huesca Sañudo, used with permission

Edited and designed by Tell Tell Poetry

Printed in the United States of America

First Printing, 2023

For Josh, Sharlie, Lady Liberty, and me

Contents

III.

Acknowledgments

I would like to thank the teachers, friends, and family who set me on this path. Always a positive influence, Mrs. Cross, your classes on literature and language set me up for a life of reading and reveling in the nuance present on the page. To the others since eighth grade, who kicked me out of their classes, I guess I made something of those lessons.

Many thanks to my parents, who only recently found out that I am a poet with a dream of publishing. For you, I capture moments sitting near the basement fire, restless sleep in a Nevada mining town, and sitting at many a table or desk worrying over relationships that never amounted to much.

To my wife and daughters, who believe that I really can achieve anything: thank you for your love and support.

Thanks to the team at Tell Tell Poetry for giving me structure to achieve this dream. Thanks to OIIOOI for the striking cover art which helped me to look both inside and out, focusing on how moving art can tell a story without words. To the universe for the experiences that have taught me and helped me grow, thank you.

To you, reader, for enjoying a work that encapsulates some of my joy and despair, for joining me through the introspection and meditations, for being willing to walk just a few steps in my shoes—I am grateful for you. Thank you for being willing to embark on this journey. May there be many more in poetry or prose!

A Glimpse

I.

Fool

I am foolish, yet wise
Careful, yet hasty
Large, yet small
True, yet false
Good, yet evil

I am not perfect, nor am I bad

I love, I learn, I live
Yet what do you think of me?

You, the only variable for me
The only thing I can't see
The only one

Much

I know much
I say much
I am much

What is much?
A measure of nothing
An experience, a feeling

Why? Why is there much?
Why is there love?
Why is there hate?
Why, why, why?

I have none, am nothing

I am not, I have not

We know power
Yet
We refuse it

We know much
Yet
We refuse it

Let it speak for itself
Let us seek for ourselves

There is hope
There is light
Keep running down the road of life

You will make it

Never forget you did not get you there

You were, nor are you, alone. They, we, are with you

Always, be not afraid

Thoughts

One day as I sat in a chair
With all these thoughts tangling my hair

Life looked at me, a cold, blank, half-formed stare
Then he asked me, *Where?*

I turned to see a world lost in thought
I began to understand, focus to my own path wrought

Those thoughts returned to me, driving me
Those things that fold and bend the mind
Those simple little forces

I realized through time and trials,
Life will always ask me

Where?

Hounds

When thoughts lose their bounds

My sanity devoured by hounds

The more I think, the less I understand

The more I know, the less sane I get

The more people don't understand, the less I try

Life is waiting there, ready to mug you

Why give it the chance?

Exertus Insania

I have loved
I have lost

I have succeeded
I have failed

We have lived
Conquered
Fallen

We know truth
It proves us

We value life
It saves us

We must kneel to be king
Live life only as we see it
There is much more, and none
There is all joy and total sorrow
Let us be

Seek

Give this, your time gone past
An afterthought, a second glimpse

See me now in verse expanded
Look where wound has healed and gone
See into my heart and soul
Hear how living whispers speak

Seek the truth unbroken
Hear the day long ring
See forever beauty
And let your mind's eye sing

Give learning, knowledge, and people
Time to sprout and grow
Seeds nestled deep in earth
Not just strewn out where you sow

Thing

You would not give a care
If I went and disappeared

You would rejoice
You would sing
You have left me a broken thing

Dangerous Skies

I see the distant
Milling clouds
They flutter, fume
I see more like them
Take human form, descending
Reaching out, grazing the horizon
The fear rushes through me

All I can see are the lies
Caught in your pretty little eyes

The clouds approach
The rain appears
The people all run in fear
I stand and contend the storm
I see peace it cannot bring
It disappears into a moonlit night

You spin, twirl
You make me smile

I walk away
A summer's day
I end the fear
That entered here

I sail the ship
And take my sip

Hemlock's bittersweet embrace

But those lies
Haunt my eyes

I'll Never Be Him

Is it just me
Who took this long to see
I'll never be the one by your side
Being your guide?

I only saw the mirage
I most desperately wanted.

The distance run
In so short a time.
This mile a simple distance—
The time it took to get to you.
I fell and saw the truth.

This revelation
The reality, not fantasy.

I'll never be him.
If only this was the other way:
Him on the outside looking in
Wishing to be the same as me.

Can you see what I mean
I just wanted my dreams.

But as this time flies by
The mile run, another fall,

I can only see the truth—
This ordinary simple thing.

I give up now
I can run no more.

These bruises won't heal
My heart won't be whole again.

Life has given me
A different path

And it won't be with you.

Half-Whole Heart

What other way is it supposed to be
With all these pieces of me

I gave you one
It broke my heart
My once-whole heart

Where did it ever go?
Is it lost forever?

Now I live lost in this place
Searching and seeking for grace

I found a bit
I savored it

I gave you some
It gave me peace
My once-whole heart

Where did it ever go?
Did I forget it? Never

Can you see
What happened to me

I gave it to you
It broke my heart
My once-whole heart

Where did it ever go?
If only I could know—

Traveling down a winding path
Looking for a shorter way

You gave me light
It gave me delight
My once-whole heart

Where did it go?

What If You Lost Everything You Knew

draw me in
throw me away
engage your fear
spare a tear

drown the memories

in the dark silence
I look away
a terrible grin
strikes my face

life caught me
by surprise
a torrent
a storm

above ever-deepening shadows
through brightening day
in the rays of brand-new light
on the glow of a moonlit night

throw me away
take it apart

end me now
don't let me take another breath

I can't see what's in store for me

would you please
throw me away

it's so broken now
I don't know why I'm living

if you don't say it
I will
I'd hate for you to kill

kill my heart
before love grows

my heart
it slows

In a Moment

Hesitation, commiseration
Won't let me leave this station

Fighting, writing
Nothing to do, I'm dying

Give me one word, just another phrase
I'm speaking slowly, nothing escaping
It's no wonder, stringing me along for days

Don't you mind, the time has passed
Simple pleasure, my heart will cry
I won't relinquish, only hold doubt

It's never over, until
In one fell swoop, the actor plays
The curtains fall
The shadows creep

The day, at last
A little respite

Never repeat what once was golden
All I know is that it's broken

Glorious, glorious day
It stretches on into the marbled sky
Into the river
That never runs dry

If the World Is Burning

If the world is burning
Where can we run?
If it feels like this
What have we done?

You've torn me up
I'm dying inside
I'm losing control
Of my life.

If my head is spinning
How do I live?
If I can't find comfort
What did I give?

Don't give in
Don't lose it all today
Don't set the world on fire
Don't just say

I can't take this anymore
I can't stand the way I live
I don't want to face the choices
Just let me give in

Don't let the world burn

'Cause if it's up in flames
Where do we turn?

Drowning

here it comes
I'm drowning again

the feelings repeating
emotions take control

the edge of reality
slipping ever closer

the difference of
a brand-new day

oh, listen to me!
I'm caught in the current
taken downstream
rushing away

I'm unconscious
dipping in the water
losing sight of you
drowning again

there it goes
I'm losing again

the memories repeating
thoughts in control

the mists of pain
hanging right above

the difference is that
I'm breathing still

don't listen to me
I'm lost in my thoughts
taken off-guard
losing again

I'm happy
surviving best I can
losing sight
losing again

I can see
through the water
I can't see
through the pain

don't let me drown
I need you here,
but without you
I'll live another day

I am
happy, happy is what I'll say

Shattered

A broken human yearning for things long past
My heart left on the table without a second glance

I left without a heavy heart
But then it was lost, never certain where it went

Been There

I wish I were perfect
Not a hair askew
Like the morning dew

I wish I were perfect
Every bursting muscle, too
Yes, that's quite a few

I wish I were perfect
Maybe 6'2"

I wish I were perfect
Every sentence true
My eyes deep blue

I wish I were perfect
      Just like you

Swell Gel

Isn't it swell when my hair is gelled
It fits as we sit and talk about this
We can't seem to go, and I'd love you to stay
The words seem hard, and you know what to say
You're perfect for me, every time we kiss
It seems so perfect just because we fit
Be yourself, you know what to do
I love our journey and I'm more in love with you

As you can see, we aren't yet tempest-tossed
In a year or two it may be lost

In the end it wasn't well
But at the time it did seem swell

If I Just Had One Shot

I knew I could be anything I wanted
I started thinking
              dreaming
                   scheming
I knew I could be anything
A robot traveler in space, searching out another race
A policeman, truer than true
A firefighter, living, breathing, as fragile as the flame
What am I?
More than I wished?
A son, a child, an heir.

Random Generation

Stiff and shift
.gif and gift
Random repeat, all is bliss

Poem this, poem that
All I think is, *oh, drat*

Never-ending, cycle low
Look there, I just saw a crow
Growing, sowing, let it go
All we are, fate bestows

Simple pleasure, pumpkin pie
You are the apple of my eye

Sand, cement and garden tower
Oh, can't you see how late the hour!

Now it's beating, we're repeating
Isn't it great, how this goes?
I just hope it doesn't show

Always be a step behind
Then you'll catch them with your mind

Just remember all it takes
Is for you to want a break

Pleasure this, pleasure that
No, I don't think you look fat

Keep it rolling, let it be
Now then here's the end, you'll see:

END

Black Ink Mirror

I write to relieve
Heart
Soul
Life
This is me

This pen a
Test
Friend
Counselor
Brother
Teacher

Hearken back to youth, those troubled years
Striving to soothe, only to be rejected

Verses written for you
In inky mirror all I see:
My own image returned

Black, my soul on paper
Yet unblemished it stands

The Red Pen

This red pen
The tool of my demise

The very one who will bring me down
I say too much

It knows me well
This pen is an inner part of me

It is my heart made plastic
My heart in ink

This page the whole world
Outside of it nothing matters to me

I write and write
And still it flows

I hope forever
All eternity

That it will never end
For after that will I silent go

Parties

I don't live for freedom
I'm not steeped in oppression
Throw tea to the harbors, but remember the victim

Browbeat the crowd, left and right, what we sell them
Inundate with news, weaken views, passion's in fashion
Turn it off, we can stop the congress in session

Emptied mags deepen crags that have always been forming
Sell 'em what's relevant, give 'em hell for that elephant
An ass what we make, it ain't free if they take it
Power and possession not far from the fray
Badge and a gun, all that matter today

Independence from what? A mythic intruder
We aren't growing up, just getting louder and ruder
Dicing for strength and constitution saves
Try it, as we amend in waves
Fix what's broken, that's the way we remain
Whole
Undivided
A nation

Revelation

I float in a dark room
I reach for anything
I'm floating anchorless

Suddenly I feel something solid
Grasping with all my might
It's too late, gravity's got hold

I hit—
Realization
I'm saved—
Found my anchor

I've lived too short to know
I've given too little to know
I've always come in second

I strike
Take my stand
I've won
Free at last

Living in a deep stupor
Living for what I have known
Living life is worth so much

Where did the dark space go?
What did I do right?
Why did I stand up and fight?

How will I end this out?

I fall
Through time and place
I'm dreaming
Of the changes

People change
But am I fighting

There is new reality
Where is mine now?
Let the happiness go

I cry
Heartbroken
I'm reeling
My tears hit sea

My head splits open
My life spills out
The river of pages carries me
A crumpled husk, I am no more

Now unbound, I float amidst stars
I see that same unending void
I see light somewhere distant
I'm swept on

I drift
Into the torrent of my fears
I'm swimming
Through the river of tears

I reach the light
I see my anchor
I feel my life slip back into my frame

The days go on
The people change

The people all are gone
As I stand on stage

Life worth living
Is worth the effort

Death worth dying
Is worth the try

And I won't cry
I won't cry

I'll laugh
I'll be
I'll see

Sample

Life unexposed
A wall.

Give no one a chance
To see your core.

Give secrets. Let your
Wall come down.

Learn from pain and
Try to see.

Where I Am From

I'm from classical music
And rock music too
I am from drums
And the violin

From Dvorak to Rush
Vivaldi to The Pillows
I'm from easy flowing, peaceful
To rock your socks off

I'm from choirs
And songs
Chocolate cake
Boxes of memories
And stacks of books

I'm from far, far away
Iceland and China
England too
I'm from green, cut grass
And neat gardens
I'm from good food
And family

I'm from my grandpa's birthday
And out of state
Shut the door!
And *Clean that plate!*
Life has taught me much
Broken me too
But most of all, I can share it here with you

Wonderdrug

All the pain
You give
All the joy makes me the same
But I am changed

The damage your wrecking ball has caused

What can I say?
There is more to it than that
The peace I feel inside
The wonderdrug of the broken

You give life and purpose
You see me through
My weirder ways

I give you what little I can
A prize not worth the effort
You continue to give me peace

With more happiness than ever before
I live these days longer
Writing my broken thoughts
My trashed dreams

My brain spills out on paper

The paper drinks in the
Nonsense, and gives me this
Another song, another poem
Another memory, to be recorded forever

You see that patience here
Has lifted me up
All this time
So little real

I am not who I once was

I am different now
I am better now
I am happy now

Give Up on Giving Up

I sit and stare and see
Life is searching, but may never find
If I never moved, life is blind
Might as well cry, or die

But why, there is so much more for me
There is so much more for all of us
Yet we run from it, we try to make it ourselves
It will never work. Giving that up now is peace.

Goodbye

To friends, goodbye
Goodbye good friends

I will long remember. Remember me too

Keep your life in your hands
Live your life well
See what you should
Say what you should

Goodbye

II.

When Did I Install a Door, I Thought I Just Had Windows

With all life knocking at my door

Many people saying more

I must head back into the fray
And send my hands into the clay
Warm and fertile at the banks
Slowly now

Sloshing along with grit that's fine
Molded up into a vase

Look and you will see, not through glass darkly
But illuminated

A masterpiece, where once was earth
You were formed and given birth

Me

I think to feel of how I lost

The one so softly spoken, rose up and took my place

But left the chain unbroken
I lost myself, but now I have become

Me

Humanity

All our problems

All our weaknesses

All our failures

All our solutions

All our strengths

All our successes:

All our humanity

Blank New Page

I travel along a familiar road
I stop to see the beauty
The valley falls away
Ascending into lavender peaks
Touching a tangerine sky

I look farther
I see the sun decay
I look deeper
I see the moon array

I travel farther
I see more splendor
I travel deeper
I look with wonder

I see this page coming back to me
A blank empty page

Waiting for a new adventure
I say it takes another day
I'm looking for another way

The page blinks back at me
It can see I have much more
Much more to tell

I may have escaped another day
I try to capture as best I can
Something drives me
A force full of happiness
I am more than I can be

I work harder
I have more joy
There *is* more joy

You see the perfect future
I look as hard as I can
You see the perfect past
I hope there is more for me

Life gets better
Step by step
I see wonders
Step by step

I arrive back on the path
Peace
A new page filled in

Another pristine page blinks at me
It asks for another adventure

No more ideas
All the experiences
Spilled out of my head
Alone with this blank page
To struggle with another day

A Picture

A half-beat tune played along
I wrote in pain, the song

I felt in peace
The wayward cry of my heart
I know it wouldn't be smart

Much better to lose
Than to never know what life is all about

To your friends
You give it all
As you begin to falter

I catch you
I wish I only knew
That same feeling they do

Can you tell me
Why I cry into the paper
My red stroked tears—

How I can feel the pain
How it stains these pages

These strokes all for you

An image, not of art
But of a broken, fragmented part:
The picture of my heart

Everything

I would have given everything for you
I can't seem to let you know
Just how much I feel

I can't come to say it
I can't display it
I want you to know
I love you so

I can't speak it a better way
I know you continue to say
Someday

We'll never be
I can see
Maybe as friends this can last

I'll keep trying to show you love
You'll say we're friends
Until the end

Clearheaded

I'm resting here
My mind is clear
A placid lake above the clouds
Eyelids shut and ears aroused
Music and words
Wash over me
As a babbling brook on rocks
Winds to a waterfall

I'm thinking
About you, about me
And everything in between

It's cold outside
A woolen snowfall
It's warm in here
Gas alight
It's great
To have my mind empty and clear

I'm singing
It's not just to myself
But I'm not singing
For anyone to hear

I take some time
To slow down

I'm breathing in
Much slower now

But I'm still resting
With my mind clear, thinking
Thinking about you

Ending

That's not the way I see this ending
There is no crash
No rash explosion
No death
No decay
It's calm and peaceful there

It may be dark and solitary and cold
But not quite lonely
'Cause really, you're not alone

It's definitely a relief and a new beginning
But there is still something there
It was never left behind

There are no pieces falling apart
You've mended your broken heart
And most everything has lost its sting

Pain may linger
But you're getting better
You've figured everything out

That may be quite the ending
For us, the boring sort
You'll be calm and peaceful there
And everything will be alright

So Much Depends

so much depends
upon

your crystalline, effortless
smile

always ready to
burst

brightening even dark
days

Mirror

the picture of the future
can be cloudy, covered in mist

but in your eyes, I see it
perfect, like an infinite mirror

Smile

What happens to the smile suspended?

Does it grow
Like a flower in spring?
Or fade—
And disappear?
Does it keep you on your feet?
Or does it wonder—
Like Galileo looking at the stars?

Maybe it just remains
Like an ancient scar.

Or does it shatter?

You

The warm embrace
The bright smile
Ushers forward feelings

The simplest look
The lightest touch
Reminds me

Your presence
Makes everything
Wonderful

Memory

Bask in beauty
Knowledge
Melody

Live with love
Compassion
Charity

See how others
Feel
Act

Give of yourself

Hear what you have done

Remember this, your lonely friend

III.

Nothingness

We live on the verge of total nothingness
All we need do is sit and stare

Those around us that see things clearly
are the only ones whom we mistrust

Life is a whirling roller coaster of death for the normal among us

Knowledge

All people know

Few people hear

I know and hear

I am no better, though
I know the needling fears
The doubts and anguish

Life batters us with surprises
Sometime as gifts
It presents bumps and bruises
The knowledge of winding ways

Knowledge is power. Share it well

Highway

Running down a narrow road
Finding peace in my own way

Cars are passing by
Some stop to ask why

I tell them all
But there is some
I couldn't say

They pass
I feel relieved
Life has given back

I'm running down this road of strife
Showing all the passersby my life

They may cheer or hiss
But I can't care less

My choices are my own
I live this life well

I see my dreams surrounding me
Apparitions, dark and fun

I see the adventures
They would take me on

They all beg of me different things

I take flight
Only one gets wings

We soar
We roar
Forevermore

I'm flying above this road of strife

My dream and I
Fly so very high

We reach the sun
This dream is done

I'm falling fast
My dream won't last

I reach for safe ground
My heart begins to pound

I can see you not so very distant
I can reach you in less than an instant

The world disappears
As the ground nears

You catch me
You lift me up
We stumble together

I'm stumbling down this road of strife
Telling you about my life

I hear you cheer
I can't care more

These choices are my own
I am ready to own them

My heart stops
Time stands still

Life goes on

Dream 1

My thoughts talk to me
They whisper things I never say

I feel their emotions
Flowing through me

I see their eyes burn
Colors of the rainbow

I see their shadows
Fusing with my own

I live their dreams
I am their reality

Dream 2

How happy it would seem
To be caught in a dream

To be in a world where life was better

The weather would be cool
We'd have no need for a pool

We would lounge about
Dreaming up new worlds

Each world better than the rest

Because as we see it
What we want is most

And then we realize
That the time we have spent
Could have been our last
And you are important in
More than your own eyes.

Broken

When the wind of broken dreams
Torn and tattered, falls

When the chill of reality
Cuts us all—

When the tears spill
On paths we crawl—

When in our life
We seem to stall,

Living seems beyond
Our call

We can't escape
But we can fall
Into the arms of our friends
And the hope that brings
Will give us wings
And again, we soar

Come let us fly together
Into eternity
Let's be friends
Just you and I
Forever you and I

Light

The greatest and most magnificent thing

The way to see on straight and narrow paths

The beacon to the lost

One hope, the belief that all is well

Light is charity
Light is love

Let all see and know it

Love

Seek the words
The thoughts
The good
Learn the truth
Know your path
Live the right
Love your neighbor

Dream 3

I never like to leave you
I'll never want to let you go

My heart screams
What do I say?

You make me better
You build me up

Don't fall apart
I don't want to find all the pieces
I'll mend what is broken
I will be there

Dream 4

The light takes hold
The darkness dies

I see your eyes
I don't know what you feel inside
I'd like to help you make it better

We sit side by side
I would love it to be true
To be the one for you

Vision clouded, my thoughts so vague
I never know
How to change

I know it's not the end

Figured Out

Now the road doesn't seem so long
It's all grown rather straight, I think
I want to say I see it all

It's so nice to feel this way
Admit it, everything so great
I'm happy to greet each new day

Beyond

Rising beyond the call of peace

Risen in the purple east

Giving light to those which fall

Raising me beyond my all

Orchid

Plumb the depths, you little wonder
Drive the azure waves asunder
Breathing in the life from surface
White-capped peaks whirl like a dervish

Golds and browns
Greens and reds
Every hill and valley covered

Fish are swimming to and fro
Where do those bubbles go—

The waves divide and crash, combining
Simple days in sun and spray
Red on skin and sunburn thriving
An effervescent, diving bay

Peace 1

I look in your eyes
All I can see
The peace therein lies
That peace is in me

Peace 2

Your eyes
Are the color of peace
The emotions in them
My happy place

Your smile
Bright, like the glistening ice
The power within
Enough to calm

Your heart
Is mine, as mine is yours
Forever side by side

Peace 3

Dark, alone
Peace and warmth
Your hand in mine

Quiet, wonderful
We embrace
Time stands still

Our first kiss,
Perfect

Clouds

Then let us go, you and I,
The farther we go the faster we fly
The wind takes us
Time, it makes us
Just like the clouds in the sky

Full at Length

Brush the ashes from the floor
Welcome every creature at your door
Comfort each beyond its own
Through this shall each receive its throne

Sweep the webs from the path
Allow in the light for this day
Erase the haggard, jagged marks
Overcoming the mistakes of the dark

Clear the fears from the mind
Invite faith, beyond that within you'd find
Sow moments of truth and right
One day to reap within the light

Release the tears from the heart
Entice serenity from at the start
Praise in heart, might, mind, and strength
Then will your joy be full at length

Away We Go

Let us go then, you and I
Travel distances through stars
Through my mind and much beyond
Farther than I've ever gone

Now amidst the deepest black
And all the brightest stars
We lie down and rest our heads
The clouds above us make
Shapes of dragons, lions, and eyes

Now we snap back, and it's a
Green spring day, warm and beautiful
The smell of life is in the air
And it can take us anywhere

In the room there sits a man
With his old and weathered hands
Yanking to and fro to clear a stump
Ratchet and keyboard freed from maw
The lion close but not abandoned
Plot and story in the cabin

Now take us back above the
Stars, through the clouds and back
To the homes we know and love
Our friends and family there

Remember the adventure, though
We will go again someday
Among the clouds above the stars
In the dark and on the grass

The Journey

I'm in a starlit room
A place short on light
I see the space expanding
As I wake, I feel

Lights explode around me
Different sounds surround me
I see a darker space
A ways down, in a quieter place

There, I see it now
A shorter distance
A different end
A new lit path

The moon hangs above
As I drift into the stars
I float away
Tasting new realities, but

As I greet a brand-new day
The noises come rushing on
I keep searching for
That distant, dark mystery

I am alone here fighting off the real
I throw away that broken, wasted part
I have found
A new heart, but

In the end
All I can need
All I can see
Is you

Life is changing
The world arraigning
The people see
The people be

I see it clearly now—
What?

I see you
I see you
I see you

Belief: Light, Love, Forever

Light, more than I know:
Beautiful, helpful, kind, hopeful

Filled with light for all eternity
Forever, longer than long

No beginning or end

I've barely been gone, but soon I will be back
Love will take me there

Give me a flame, a spark
Let me give you light

I can't give you everything, but I can give you what I know

Here, take it further for me
Grow it bigger for me
Build a bonfire of light so everyone can take a little for themselves
Then I will be happy

One spark can save us all

.

Notes

Many of these poems take their inspiration from the music and lyrics of the following:

"Dangerous Skies" draws cadence inspiration from "War?" by System of a Down.

"Half-Whole Heart," in referencing pieces of a heart in line with further motifs, also encourages a reference to "Pieces," by Sum 41.

"In a Moment" draws initial cadence inspiration from "War?" by System of a Down and alludes to the lyrics of "Wine Red," by The Hush Sound, later in the verse. The line "It's no wonder, stringing me along for days" is an allusion to "Lovesong," by The Cure.

"If the World is Burning" was imagined in part under the influence of "Afterlife," by Avenged Sevenfold.

"If I Just Had One Shot" is clearly a response to "Lose Yourself," by Eminem.

"Parties" draws inspiration from "Close Your Eyes (And Count to Fuck)," by Run the Jewels, with a nod to Zack de la Rocha.

"So Much Depends" takes its inspiration and form from William Carlos Williams's "The Red Wheelbarrow."

"Smile" takes its inspiration and form from Langston Hughes's "Harlem."

"Octopus's Garden," by The Beatles is evoked in the lines of "Dream 2."

The last line of "Broken" shares a feeling with the bridge in "Check Yes, Juliet," by We the Kings.

The first lines of "Clouds" and "Away We Go" are in homage to T.S. Eliot.

About the Author

J Brian Andersen was born in a small Southern California town, but he has no memories of the months there before moving with the family to other states. Due to these shallow roots, he grew up everywhere and is no stranger to travel. At the ripe old age of thirty, he resides in Taiwan with his wife and two daughters, where he seeks to  enjoy life. With a penchant for listening to audiobooks and 80s punk, you're likely to find headphones on him regardless of the activities going on in his vicinity. The evolution from Gregorian chant and boys' choirs from his early years adds to the liturgical nature of Andersen's poems. You will likely find subtle nods to influential musicians and historical events strewn throughout both his poetry and prose.